4/15

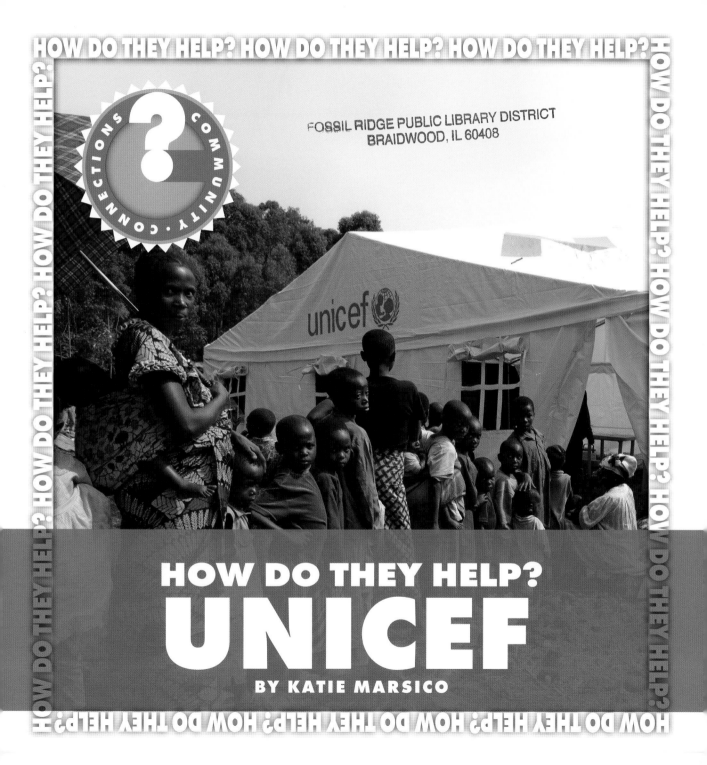

COMMUNITY · CONNECTIONS

# HOW DO THEY HELP?
# UNICEF
## BY KATIE MARSICO

CHERRY LAKE Publishing

Published in the United States of America by Cherry Lake Publishing
Ann Arbor, Michigan
www.cherrylakepublishing.com

Content Adviser: Cynthia Rathinasamy, Master of Public Policy, Concentration in International Development, Gerald R. Ford School of Public Policy, The University of Michigan, Ann Arbor, MI
Reading Adviser: Marla Conn, ReadAbility, Inc.

Photo Credits: ©Julien Harneis/http://www.flickr.com/CC-BY-SA 2.0, cover, 1, 7, 15, 21; ©UN Photo/Jean Pierre Laffont, 5; ©Pierre Holtz for UNICEF/www.hdptcar.net/ http://www.flickr.com/CC-BY-2.0, 9; ©UN Photo/GG, 11; ©evan wheeler/ http://www.flickr.com/CC-BY-SA 2.0, 13; ©UN Photo/Evan Schneider,17; ©UN Photo/Eskinder Debebe, 19

**LIBRARY OF CONGRESS CATALOGING-IN-PUBLICATION DATA**
Marsico, Katie, 1980-
  The United Nations Children's Fund (UNICEF) / by Katie Marsico.
    pages cm. — (Community connections)
  Includes bibliographical references and index.
  ISBN 978-1-63188-031-5 (hardcover) — ISBN 978-1-63188-117-6 (pdf) — ISBN 978-1-63188-074-2 (pbk.) — ISBN 978-1-63188-160-2 (ebook)
  1. UNICEF–Juvenile literature. I. Title.
  HV703.M37 2015
  362.7—dc23                    2014006220

Cherry Lake Publishing would like to acknowledge the work of The Partnership for 21st Century Skills. Please visit www.p21.org for more information.

Printed in the United States of America
Corporate Graphics Inc.

# CONTENTS

HOW DO THEY HELP?

# WORKING FOR WOMEN AND CHILDREN

For child workers in the Central American nation of Belize, there is little time to play. Some work on farms where they often use dangerous tools and chemicals. Others are forced to commit crimes to earn money.

Around the world an estimated 115 million children are working.

4

Some children are forced to work, so they can earn money for their families.

THINK!

Think about what your life would be like if you worked long hours every day after school. Imagine working so much that you didn't get to attend school at all! How do you think being a child laborer would affect your future?

Fortunately, organizations such as the United Nations Children's Fund (UNICEF) are trying to help children in these dangerous situations.

UNICEF raises awareness about how child labor destroys individual lives, as well as entire communities.

This organization is part of the United Nations (UN). UNICEF creates programs that support the health, safety, and education of women and children worldwide. They often work in areas affected by **poverty**.

UNICEF gives school supplies to students who need them.

Are you able to guess what the UN is? If you said it's an **international** organization, you'd be right! The UN is a group of 193 world nations, including Canada and the United States.

UNICEF's programs protect women and children from abuse, violence, and **discrimination**. UNICEF helps communities provide food and basic health care, too. It also tries to make sure that all children have equal opportunities to attend school.

Finally, UNICEF offers emergency aid, or assistance. Its goal is to keep women and children safe and well, even during times of war and disaster.

UNICEF helps care for sick children such as this girl.

## LOOK!

Go online with a
parent, teacher, or
other adult. Look for
photos of UNICEF
operations around the
globe. What services
do you see UNICEF
providing to different
communities?

9

# THE PAST AND PRESENT

The history of UNICEF dates back to 1946. World War II was over but had caused widespread hunger and disease throughout Europe. The UN created UNICEF to focus on caring for women and children affected by these problems.

UNICEF helped provide food, clothing, and medicine. Yet UN leaders knew that women and

UNICEF makes sure that children around the world have enough food to survive.

What effects do wars have on children? Ask your teacher what dangers young people living in modern war zones face.

children elsewhere would need aid and protection in the future. So they decided to make UNICEF a permanent organization in 1953.

Today, UNICEF programs exist in more than 190 countries and territories all over the world. They allow millions of people to lead healthier lives.

About 11,500 employees have jobs with UNICEF. They represent many different nations.

UNICEF workers prepare **donations** for people in need.

Are you able to guess how UNICEF pays for its many international programs? National governments provide two-thirds of UNICEF's funding. Private organizations, companies, and individuals supply the rest. They do this by making donations.

13

Some workers educate government officials about issues affecting women and children in **developing countries**. They encourage lawmakers to make decisions that support UNICEF's goals.

People involved in UNICEF have other jobs, too. They might be doctors, **sanitation** experts, or teachers. Other employees conduct studies about international problems that women and children face.

People in need line up to receive UNICEF aid.

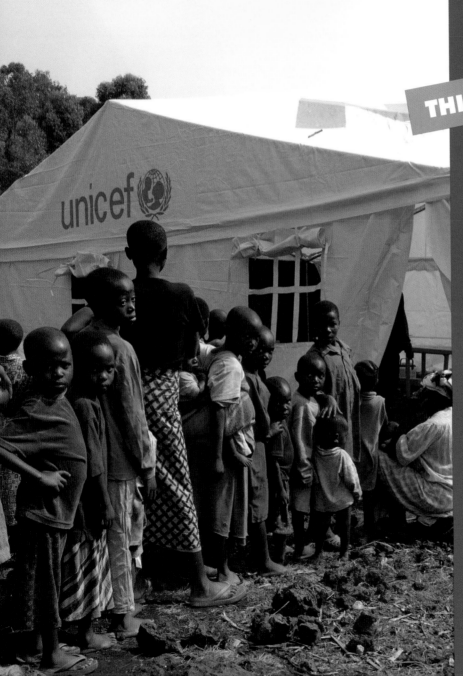

Think about what it takes to work with UNICEF. This group runs sites all over the world. So, it's helpful for employees to know as many languages as possible.

# AMAZING EFFORTS

In some cases, UNICEF gives poor families a small allowance to pay for basic things they need to live. In other situations, it funds health care services. UNICEF helps provide women and children with **vaccinations**.

It also supplies struggling communities with medicine, vitamins, and fresh water. UNICEF works to improve

Some families pump their own water from the ground every day.

How does better sanitation lead to better health for women and children? Learn the answer by talking to any doctors, nurses, or community leaders you know.

sanitation, too. This involves everything from laying pipes to finding better ways to manage waste.

Other UNICEF efforts involve working with schools to make sure that all children have a chance to learn. This is especially important in areas where girls or students with special needs face unfair treatment. UNICEF also encourages governments

In some countries, girls aren't allowed to attend school, but UNICEF supports education for everyone.

## LOOK!

Ask an adult to help you search the Internet for pictures of school programs supported by UNICEF. Do you see any similarities to your own classroom? What differences do you notice?

19

to strengthen laws that protect women and children from abuse and discrimination.

Such problems are more likely to occur during war and disaster. That's why UNICEF offers emergency services. Thanks to UNICEF's efforts, women and children everywhere live in a safer, healthier world.

Because of UNICEF, this child lives a healthier life.

Create your own UNICEF fundraiser! Ask a parent or teacher to help you review the organization's Web site. Then decide how you plan to raise money for UNICEF. A school bake sale and community car wash are just a few possibilities!

21

# GLOSSARY

**developing countries** (dih-VEH-luh-ping KUHN-treez) countries that are often poor and that are working to develop more modern businesses and social practices

**discrimination** (dis-krih-muh-NAY-shuhn) the act of treating a person or group unfairly because of their beliefs, background, or physical differences

**donations** (doh-NAY-shuhnz) money, food, clothes, or other items that are given to help someone in need

**international** (in-tuhr-NAH-shuh-nuhl) involving two or more countries

**poverty** (PAH-vuhr-tee) the state of being poor

**sanitation** (sah-nuh-TAY-shuhn) conditions related to public health

**vaccinations** (vak-suh-NAY-shuhnz) shots or drops taken by mouth that protect people against various diseases

# FIND OUT MORE

## BOOKS

Anderson, Judith, and Christian Aid (contributor). *An Equal Chance for Girls and Women*. Mankato, MN: Sea-to-Sea, 2010.

Brownlie Bojang, Ali. *Aid and Development*. Mankato, MN: Black Rabbit Books, 2009.

Connolly, Sean. *UNICEF*. Mankato, MN: Smart Apple Media, 2009.

## WEB SITES

### Human Rights Education Associates (HREA)—Simplified Version of the Convention on the Rights of the Child
*www.hrea.org/feature-events/simplified-crc.html*
Visit this Web site for a list of basic rights the UN guarantees every child.

### Trick-or-Treat for UNICEF: Clubs and Groups
*www.trickortreatforunicef.org/clubs-groups*
Check out this Web page to learn how school groups and clubs raise money for UNICEF every fall.

# INDEX

## ABOUT THE AUTHOR

Katie Marsico is the author of more than 150 children's books. She lives in a suburb of Chicago, Illinois, with her husband and children.